LIFE WITH AND WITHOUT GOD

Life With
AND
Without God

TIMOTHY PAUL BELFORD

Designed by: Vince Pannullo
Printed in the United States of America by
One Communications LLC 800-621-2556

ISBN:978-0-578-28905-2

CONTENTS

DEDICATION

THIS book is dedicated to my best friend and brother. To the one who left heaven to give His life for me. To The King of Kings and Lord of Lords, The Alpha and Omega, The Beginning and the End. The one before whom every knee will bow, and every tongue confess. He is Jesus Christ the Righteous, The Holy One of God.

You will keep him in
PERFECT
PEACE
WHOSE MIND IS
STAYED ON YOU
because he trusts in you
ISAIAH 26:3

INTRO

I wrote this book to document what has taken place both inside and outside of myself. Based on true life experience and years of personal suffering, this book is aimed at people feeling helpless, hopeless, and lost. It is aimed at anyone with a hunger for the true and living God and to those feeling trapped in empty, works-oriented, or lifeless belief systems. It is designed to bring comfort to those who suffer in the arena of the mind and to help make the person of Jesus Christ more accessible to individuals whose thought processes make their lives difficult. It is for those seeking an inner peace away from the suffering of guilt, despondency, and depression.

This book is a guide to Christ for the unhappy, the uncertain and the unloved. It is an open invitation to glimpse into the suffering of one man's soul and the path out of emotional distress. It chronicles the profound effects of disease and despair, of loneliness and melancholy. It is the culmination of thought and experience. It is an illustration of correction and learning. It reflects deep wounds and necessary healing. It portrays capability and inability. It displays both brokenness and wholeness. It is a type of life story without consistent chronology. It is a trip on and off the not-so-merry-go-round of self. It is the journey of a speck of dust seeking its way toward God and walking together with the willing.

CHAPTER ONE

MY STORY

I was born in the year 1961 at St. Michael's Hospital in Newark, N.J. and lived in Elizabeth with my parents until the age of two. At that time, we moved to Long Branch, a popular town on the Jersey Shore. I was the eldest of two children. My father Milton was a high school mathematics teacher, and my mother Elaine was a grade-school teacher. My younger sister Alison eventually followed in my parent's footsteps and too became a teacher.

Education was not my thing; I was never a very good student. Growing up I had lots of friends, played sports, and loved spending hours in the woods exploring, learning and critter catching. But unfortunately, my family would not be exempt from its share of sorrows. One of my earliest memories is the death of my baby sister. It is the first time I can remember praying to God. Amy died silently, choking in her car seat during a Sunday afternoon family drive after church. I'll never forget as a young boy seeing my dad utterly stricken with grief. While visiting her grave with my parents and sister one Sunday after church, I noticed a nearby gravestone that had the same last name as mine on it. It read "Peter Harrison Belford." I asked my parents about it, and they told me I had a younger brother who was stillborn. They tried one more time to have a child but tragically Brian was also stillborn. There are some things in life we will never understand, for which there are simply no answers. One summer at about the age of eleven I was at the playground when I saw the most beautiful little girl, I had ever laid eyes on. She had long dark hair and almond-shaped eyes. I had to talk to her so I got up my nerve and approached her with my first ever rap. She told me her name was Marie Ann. We talked for a while on the swings then a short time later she left. I didn't see her again that summer but I didn't forget about her. My family moved to another town in the fall and on the first day at my new school when I walked into the classroom the first face, I saw was the little girl from the playground. I couldn't believe it! She became my first little sweetheart. Unfortunately, I never got the chance to give her a first kiss as she was diagnosed with a malignant brain tumor just a short time later. During one trip home from the hospital, I gave her a jade necklace which she cherished. Sadly, Marie Ann died a short time later. This first lost love left a scar. My family moved once again but fortunately I remained in the same school system. I continued through junior high and high school but in my sophomore year I began hanging out with a different group of friends and taking drugs. I became an instant party animal, constantly drinking, drugging, and fighting. But my fights weren't normal schoolyard fights, they were eruptions of uncontrollable rage. During the summers I worked in "The Haunted Mansion" a gigantic three-story house of horrors at the Long Branch Amusement Pier. Growing up it was the best job I ever had, getting paid to dress up like a monster and scare the daylights out of people. I would return home only late at night to eat and sleep after working at the mansion all day then partying at the pier bars all night with my coworkers, a colorful crowd of actors, artists, freaks, and hippies with a security staff of local bikers.

My senior year in high school I dated a girl named Lisa. She was tall, with blond hair and hazel eyes. I'd often hitchhike from my house in Monmouth Beach to her house in West Long Branch about ten miles away. My route was Ocean Avenue to Cedar Avenue. One summer day I came upon a Foodtown tractor trailer stopped at the light with its blinker on, going right onto Cedar. In my brilliance I decided to climb onto the back of the tractor trailer and get a free ride unbeknownst to the driver. I climbed onto the back of the truck, stuck my feet in the metal step and grabbed the nylon door strap. We took off going 40 mph. It was a rough, bumpy ride and my arms quickly began to tire. Wearing only a t- shirt, cut offs and sneakers I soon realized I wasn't going to be able to hold on much longer. I was hoping to hear the air brakes engage as we approached the traffic light by Monmouth College so we could stop, and I'd be able to hop off but no such luck. My arms were giving out and it became apparent that it was decision time. I could hold on until the last second and fall off or jump off and try to use my arms to break my fall. I chose the latter, took a deep breath, and made my move. I discovered asphalt doesn't have a lot of give to it and tumbled over and over like Evil Knievel at Caesar's Palace but miraculously never hit my head and sustained no serious injuries. God had His hand on me many times in my life and this was nothing short of a miracle. When I came out of the roll I was in a standing position. All I had left was a face, the rest of me was total road rash. I flagged down the next car and the horrified driver kindly took me to my friend Neil's house nearby. Neil doused me with bottles of hydrogen peroxide in the backyard and I was a walking, talking scab for the rest of the summer. So, what did I learn from that experience? Absolutely nothing. I continued living on like a reckless idiot for decades. I know firsthand that God is merciful to fools, and He had far more mercy on me than I deserved, and He still does. Like I said, He was always with me. Sometimes I can't believe I made it to age sixty, especially when I did so much not to. After my senior year, Lisa and I broke up and my way of dealing with it was to continue with the drugs and go completely wild. At one point I attempted suicide by overdosing and cutting my wrist but thankfully once again God's merciful hand was there. I suffered from a growing depression, a sorrow that had been with me since I was a child. I would describe it as a consuming dark emptiness, a loneliness that was surfacing and growing in intensity after many years of lying dormant.

As the years went on and with the proper catalysts it would metastasize and bloom into a full-blown daily pit of despair which made me curse being alive every morning I awoke, praying each day would be my last. I cannot describe nor can long term daily depression be understood by a non-sufferer. Every morning seemed a cruel resentencing to a relentless

mantle of gloom which set its oppressive weight crush-
ingly upon my shoulders. At age 21 I was singing in a
heavy metal cover band called *Serpent.* We played all
the local clubs including Asbury Park's famous Stone
Pony and for the next few years my life was rock n'
roll, often partying till dawn after gigs. In a few years
the band eventually broke up. My family had moved
once more and after an argument with my parents
one evening I impulsively decided to hitchhike to
Florida. This was quite an experience. I remember
walking in the mountains of Virginia on the second
night of my journey, the snow falling fast and hard
with no cars in sight. When the snow reached my
knees, I started to get scared. I prayed and made God
all the standard "I'll never do it again" promises.
Then at the top of the mountain, I saw a tiny speck
of light which were headlights. I prayed as hard as
I could that I would get a ride and I did. A soldier
picked me up and drove me all the way to North
Carolina where I took a hotel room. My mother had
packed some sandwiches for me and when I went to
eat one, noticed she had wedged some twenty-dollar
bills inside. All feelings surrounding the argument
which sent me on my trip instantly vanished.

Sometime the next day I was picked up by a girl
from the mountains of South Carolina named Angie

who explained that she was on the run from her biker boyfriend and his club. This was great. I was now being chased down by a bunch of angry bikers. But thank God they never caught up. Angie and I talked a lot about God during our time together. We parted ways and I completed my journey after one or two more rides. I worked at a supermarket while in Florida and one coworker always used to tell me about his church as God was still trying to reach me. Eventually I returned to New Jersey and kept the party going. One night soon after, I remember crying out loud to God, asking him why I was alive. Almost immediately I happened to run into an old friend named John who was a born again Christian and he started telling me all about Jesus and salvation. Then it hit me. I wanted to know about God. I went to church with my old friend. The problem was that what I was being told conflicted with what was in my heart. The pastor screamed loudly on Sunday morning and told me God wanted me to be wealthy and if I wasn't that it was my fault. The poor man in the wheelchair was told his faith was weak. People were married and divorced quickly, and I was one of them.

I left that church feeling angry and bitter. After getting divorced I went on a prolonged cocaine binge and experienced a depth of depression never dealt with before. I sought relief from my depression with a therapist but sadly it was to no avail and chose instead as always to self-medicate. During my chaotic life, I had learned to use humor to cope and had always been a funny person, so I tried my hand at stand-up comedy and became fairly successful. I appeared on MTV, performed at the NYC Improv and countless other comedy clubs, co-hosted a radio show and traveled all over the country. I spent entire summers in luxurious beachfront hotels performing nightly and produced my own shows. But after fifteen years I had enough of shifty agents, traveling, hotels and the politics of the entertainment industry so I left comedy. In the early 90's I was dating a girl named Mary who lived on a hippie ranch by the beach. The relationship was volatile and full of sex and drugs. This went on for a couple of years until one night I caught her cheating on me. Her betrayal evoked the reemergence of my depression and rage. Coupled with the sorrowful hangover from my divorce, I swallowed a handful of pills in a second suicide attempt which landed me in the hospital for two weeks under psychiatric observation. Once again by His great mercy, God spared my life. After being discharged I once again returned to the only life I knew. Shortly thereafter I sought help for my substance abuse at America's Keswick, a Christian treatment facility located in Whiting, NJ. Keswick was a great experience; their caring staff was a blessing, and I met many very special people there. After nine months I successfully graduated from their wonderful, scripturally based program. Unfortunately, I did not seek follow up treatment according to their recommendations and eventually returned to my sinful ways.

After more than a decade, I was diagnosed in August 2007 with a skin disease called Lentigo, a dermal form of free radical toxicity. I chronicled my battle with Lentigo in an upcoming chapter called "The Mask." Learning about and treating the disease led me into the nutritional field and I have been working since as a nutritionist for the past fifteen years. God has used me in this capacity in ways I never imagined. I have helped countless people physically, mentally, emotionally, and spiritually. But I hadn't fully repented. Then in a complete turn of events, I was suddenly diagnosed and hospitalized from January 31 through February 6, 2021, with non-Covid double pneumonia of both lungs, sepsis, malnutrition, and dehydration. My weight went from 185 pounds to 148 pounds. They said I could easily have died. I also developed issues with my bladder and had to be catheterized three times. My pulse was monitored and at one point dropped below 85 which isn't good. Very strangely, a doctor I saw only one time came in and told the nurses to remove my supplemental oxygen at that very moment. They looked shocked but followed his orders. He then disappeared and I never saw him again. As soon as he left the room, the nurses readministered the oxygen and apologized, saying they had no idea why he would issue such a harmful directive. I have my thoughts about the reason why, but they will remain unspoken. Hospitals are places to recover from crises, they are not places to get well and thrive.

After being discharged from the hospital it took me nearly six months to recover. I took the proper vitamin supplements to increase my immune and respiratory function. Eventually I regained my strength and weight and was able to return to work. I rededicated my life to God and pursued Him with a new and steadfast determination. A dear friend came to my aid by setting up a Go Fund Me page on Facebook and through the kindness of both friends and strangers I was able to get back on my feet financially. I was also blessed by the kindness of my parents, who by God's grace are still alive and invited me to stay with them. They are in their mid-eighties, and

I was honored to be able to spend time with them and help them with things even as they were helping me. I became newly involved and reacquainted with several different ministries as well. I began volunteering once again with Aslan Youth Ministries (you can read more about Aslan in the chapter entitled "A Few Short Stories'") I started supporting Veterans for Child Rescue who work with law enforcement dismantling the satanic child trafficking networks and became a member of Heaven's Saints Motorcycle Ministry. So once again in His infinite mercy, God helped me survive what I easily may not have. All I want to do from now until He calls me home is to love and serve Him. I want my thoughts, words, and actions to be pleasing in His sight. I want to be who He created me to be and do whatever it is I'm called to do which is why I've written this book. He has used all my self-imposed suffering to reign me in and create a daily dependence on Him. He also uses it to help and comfort others who are suffering. This is where I am today, and I remain dependent on God moment by moment. Many of the moments are truly difficult. But many others are very beautiful. It all comes down to faith. Trusting God daily. Nothing more, nothing less. So that's my story...and I'm sticking to it.

THE MASK

IN August of 2007 I was diagnosed with a skin disease called Lentigo. Most people have never heard of it. But at one time or another you have probably seen older people with what are called age, sun, or liver spots. These are toxins and dead cells from within the body which clump together then emerge & form yellowish brown spots on the skin surface. It is an actual altering of the DNA. Cases of Lentigo vary from a few scattered, barely noticeable light spots to very large dark patches on the skin, often on the face. The pictures I encountered on the internet of both young and old people suffering from advanced Lentigo were disturbing to say the least. When I first viewed them, I became extremely scared, fearing the inevitability that my face would become as marred and disfigured as the people I viewed in the pictures. Initially I experienced only a few small spots on my face and shoulders. I went to doctors and dermatologists who told me there was nothing they could do. Slowly over several months the condition worsened & I developed a subsequent anxiety disorder. The fact of the matter is that I was headed for an anxiety disorder despite the Lentigo. I had been a nervous wreck for years, an angry, selfish, vain, nervous wreck. Overexposure to sunlight is the primary cause of Lentigo and I had most certainly spent too much time at the beach in the sun. There are other contributing factors such as chemical exposure, smoking etc. But excessive sunlight was undeniably the primary cause.

I watched in horror as the spots grew larger and larger. More and more spots emerged, forming strange patterns on my skin. My eyebrows and eyelashes began to fall out due to the extreme stress and anxiety I was experiencing. As a result, histamine began to build up on my face as well, blotching my skin, eroding my beard, and forming thick, dark, scab-like patches which covered large areas of my face. This was a living nightmare from which there seemed no escape. Every time I looked in the mirror, there was the mask of Lentigo looking back at me. It was not my face and yet it was. As a vain person in a culture of vanity, I was left in a vulnerable and disconnected state. The fact that the medical community possesses very little knowledge of the condition and that there is no existing medical treatment was disconcerting to say the least. Cases as severe as mine indicate that there is significant free radical activity or cellular damage occurring within the body. This is termed "free radical intoxication." It can affect some or all of the internal organs. In its most severe form, it can cause permanent deafness, destroying the cilia of the inner ear.

After about a month of living with the disease, spiraling in fear and suffering daily panic attacks without any type of relief or end in sight, my imagination had become a torture device over which I had no control. Night after sleepless night insomnia sank its tormenting claws into me. I lost over forty pounds. I grew weaker and as a result I could not function at work and eventually lost my job and apartment. I had become a victim of my own worry. But worry is unbelief. It was not disbelief but unbelief. In the Book of Mark 9:24, the demon-possessed boy's father makes a plea to Jesus: "I believe, help my unbelief." I have heard disbelief defined as the denial of God's ability to act, and unbelief the denial of God's desire to act. In scripture, Jesus repeatedly tells us not to worry. In the Sermon on the Mount. We are told not to worry about our lives, food, drink, clothing, and yet we do. Worry is simply a lack of trust. One of my favorite Scriptures is Jeremiah 17:7: "Blessed is the man who trusts in the Lord and has his confidence in Him." To trust in God and not in ourselves, is the way out of worry. The voice of my worry is getting weaker thanks to God. But to begin to defeat worry, I had to come face-to-face with worrisome circumstances. I can't deal the death blow to worry as Jesus did in the Garden of Gethsemane. But God is walking with me through the valleys of my life and helping me with my worry and my unbelief. I have always been a worrier, but I don't want to be anymore. Hebrews 11:6 says: "Without faith, it is impossible to please God" and I want to please Him. He knows what is best for me and I want to increase both my faith and trust in Him. I know he hears me when I ask for faith and trust because that is in line with His will. I tend to worry about things I am afraid of. Jesus says fear not over and over, In His Word He has given me permission to release or to let go of my worry. I have not conquered it, overpowered it or overcome it with my will but with His help I may increasingly release it to Him. It is easier to let go of something than to hold onto it. In letting go I am released from its weight. By holding on I must support its weight. In Matthew 11:28-30, Jesus said "Come to me all you who labor and are heavy laden and I will give you rest. Take My yoke upon you and learn from Me, for I am gentle and humble in spirit and in Me you will find rest for your souls. For My yolk is easy and My burden is light."

For so many years, I walked around with a heavy burden and finally it took its toll. Yet I can't look back in regret, only ahead in hope. That is the only way I can grow. Amazingly, one day for some unknown reason, the dark patches on my face suddenly peeled away and disappeared. I looked like my old self again. I was also very blessed that God led me to the right nutritionist who after analyzing my blood work, recommended all the proper supplements to cleanse my system from the free-radical toxicity and start me on the road to recovery. I must remember that this is not solely my battle but God's as well because I belong to Him. He took me to a very special place with the illness. He makes what is difficult to bear bearable, what is difficult to endure endurable, what is impossible to deal with possible. I learned something through this experience that most people never do. I went from looking normal to looking like I had AIDS. Going out in public was an interesting experience. I received looks of pity, looks of horror, and even bought a pair of reading glasses to hide behind. I learned how people who look differently must feel at times and I learned how precious the feelings of others are. I learned that I don't want to add to someone's suffering through my own ignorance or cruelty. I have experienced tremendous comfort at the hands of God in my suffering and strength from His arms which He keeps wrapped around me. I have learned to care less about what people think of me and more about what God thinks of me and the truth is, He thinks about me all the time.

I have had a continual dialog with God as He has never removed His presence from me. In fact, the more I have suffered the more I have sensed Him with me. This cannot be learned in the safety of our worldly comfort zones as we revel in their eggshell fragility. As the heavens are higher than the earth so are God's ways higher than our ways. His desire is to bring us up so to speak where He is, above that which is natural, common, and ordinary. We are created or recreated in God to be anything but natural, common or ordinary. To deny this is to deny our true selves, who we were originally designed to be in Him. God is so vast, so much other than we can know or be taught. He is beyond definition and comprehension. What we get if we are fortunate, are glimpses. Limited glimpses of the limitless God who expresses Himself in many diverse ways, through so many diverse situations and through so many diverse people. We do a great disservice to both God and ourselves when we settle for the limitation that comes from living apart from Him. On the flip side of limitation is the limitless character, nature, and love of God. I think it's sad that people unknowingly choose to live in unfulfilled limitation when God makes His limitless and completely fulfilling self so readily available. Often, we may lack the proper guide but that is not our fault. He is just a "help me" away. We can access God and His limitless love. He wants us to. He calls to us constantly, but we are often so preoccupied with our thoughts, our feelings, our lives, and ourselves that we can't hear Him.

In my case an unusual condition helped me get closer to God and I am very thankful to Him for it. The symptoms of disease may come and go but not God. He is omni-present, steadfast, and sure. He can be called upon, relied upon, leaned on and looked to. He is your strength, your shelter, your rock and your refuge. He wants to be your Father, your brother and your best friend and He loves you more than you can ever imagine.

UPS AND DOWNS

U PS and downs are a part of life. We all experience them at one time or another. Our life patterns have both highs and lows. Some people's highs and lows can be exceedingly extreme, sometimes making daily function difficult. In the psychiatric industry, the term manic has been used and sometimes overused to describe these patterns of ups and downs. The term has become part of the vernacular of our times.

Regarding ups and downs, I can think of no better biblical example than King David. In the Book of Psalms, 3:1, David speaks of how deeply troubled he is. In the Psalm 4:1, David speaks of his profound distress. In Psalm 4:7, he speaks of the gladness he now feels in his heart. In Psalm 6:3, David shares how greatly troubled his soul is. He goes on in verses 6 and 7 to express weariness and groanings, his grief and tears. In Psalm 7:1 and 2, David reveals the great fear that his enemies will literally tear him to pieces. Then in Psalm 8, David opens with uplifting, glorious praises to God and closes with the same. In Psalm 9, David's heart is soaring as he praises

God and shares his intense gladness, rejoicing and declaring his desires to tell all the people of God's marvelous works.

Then suddenly, in Psalm 10, David is questioning why God is so far from him and seems to be hiding Himself. David's expression of troubles continues to Psalm 13, which opens with David asking how long he will be forgotten by God, why God continues to remain hidden and reveals the daily sorrow of his heart. Then, just three short Psalms later in 16:9, David speaks of his once again glad heart, his glorious rejoicing, and the solace of his hope. David levels off through the next five Psalms, expressing faith, trust and the goodness of God. Then suddenly in Psalm 22:1, David opens with the prophetic cry of a broken heart, "My God, my God, why have you forsaken me?" Again, he questions why God seems so far from helping him, and why God is so far from seeing his tears and hearing his groanings, which continue day and night. David even describes himself as a worm and not as a man.

Now we segue to the classically beautiful Psalm 23, known as the "Psalm of Comfort," wherein David expresses the restoration of his soul, and his profound sense of peace and safety. Jump two quick Psalms to 25:17, and there again is David, now expressing his loneliness, affliction, his troubled heart, and inescapable distress. Now considering all these ups and down, was David manic? Hardly. The Bible describes him as a man after God's own heart. King David was not manic; he was human, just like you and me.

Save Everything

Save the dolphins, save the whales
save the turtles, save the snails
save the frogs, save the bees
save the dogs, but not the fleas.
Save the chickens, save the fish
save your breath, how I wish.
Save the ospreys, save the deer
save the children, save the tears.
Save the algae, save the moss
Springsteen stinks, he's not my boss.
Save the eagles, save the terns
save the oak trees, save the ferns.
Save the mushrooms, save the dirt
save some room for your dessert.
Save the ocean, save the springs
save the jellyfish that stings.
Save the owl, hear him screech
save your rights, protect your speech
save the tiger, save the mole
but tell me who will save your soul…

CHAPTER TWO

BC

THIS poetic chapter deals with honest intro-
spection of myself, my life and my conclusions
thereof before surrendering my life to Jesus. .

Eternal Regret -   My fear of inescapable,
unending remorse for things I hadn't done.
(James 4:17 and Matthew 25:26).

Better Off Alone - Using isolation as a means
of self-protection can lead to loneliness and
depression.
(Genesis 2:18).

The Security of Rage - Anger became an all
too familiar coping mechanism for me but it
comes with a price.
(James 1:20)

Spite - Judge not lest you be judged.
(Matt. 7:1)

Fading Echoes - When we distance ourselves from God and ignore His voice, it grows more and more faint until it is completely replaced by the voice of self.

(Jeremiah 3:14 and 3:22).

Eternal Regret

I let so many years pass by
things will be just fine, I'd sigh.
So neat and clean yet still a slob
a lazy slob without a job.

I reap the harvest of the sloth
the harvest of the lazy.
I bow my head and slurp my broth
my God I must be crazy.

Avoiding the fear of eternal regret
ungrateful for payment of eternal debt.
Captivated by the illusions of life
now I stand here alone with no children or wife.

Falsely contrite as I indulged my sin
found in places I should never have been.
Behind my back and face to face
a scared lonely rat in a lonely rat race
and I just waited.

What was it I was so long waiting for?

A friend or a hero to walk through the door?
or a Savior so gentle I would choose to ignore?
God I'm so sorry, I'm so very sorry.

Scrambling now to make up for lost time.
Scrambling now to find words that will rhyme.
Wondering if perhaps it is too late
'cuz for so many years I'd just wait and I'd wait…
Please forgive me...

BETTER OFF ALONE

Leaning on the shoulder of my shadow
it's constantly just me, myself and I.
I'm better off alone just with my shadow
there is no answer to the question why.
If I stay in my yard at least I will be safe
behind fences I know none can scale.
Half a century high, half a century wide
constructs I have designed to not fail.
Better off alone in a fortress made of doubt
nothing I have seen as yet
could ever draw me out.
And my fences and my fortress and my shadow never lie
and they never make me wonder
and they never ask me why
if they're truly necessary
or if I'd ever care to try
to live without them even for a while.
But the truth despite their safety is
they never make me smile.
Still, they keep me feeling sane
even Tarzan had his Jane
but its okay, they dull the pain
of being alone.

THE SECURITY OF RAGE

When I'm feeling vulnerable
prisoner within my cage
where no one else can touch me
the security of rage.

Here I find strength to stand alone
and I have since my young age
I seek dark sanctuary
the security of rage.

Familiar to my heart and soul
safety is my only goal
all I want is to feel whole
the security of rage.

A beaten path within my brain
the burden like a ball and chain
I know it's driving me insane
the security of rage.

But now I seek to separate
I long to turn the page

and divorce my heart and soul
from the security of rage.

My rage said to me, "Not so fast,
just remember how in times past
I gave you refuge, served you well
and paved your path straight down to hell."

Then I said to my rage
"If any man be in Christ, he is a new creation,
old things have passed away and behold,
all things have become new."

SPITE

Spite is a prison in which we sit alone.
The bars made of rights which we claim for our
own.
We are judge, we are jury
and our verdict is fury.
Because we're not as bad
as we point and accuse,
mirror, mirror, on the wall we refuse.

Fading Echoes

When I walked the futility of my own mind
I was sure I could see yet was so very blind.
As once I roamed the vast prison of my own fear
the expanse of God's freedom
I dared never draw near.
I would speak empty words from my
own foolish heart
the insane repetitions each day I would start
and just hope somehow through it
I'd find a new thing
with a roll of the dice to see what it would bring.
Frustration, regret and deep unfulfilled boredom
Completely immersed in my spiritual whoredom.
My soul I'd not sell yet I'd give it away
the truth I'd not tell only lies could I say
a loser lost in the fun of the games I would play.
Like a sheep off the cliff how I refused to hear
the voice of my Shepherd I dared never draw near.
Trained my ears to the torturing lies of a thief
the unknowing apostle of complete unbelief.
My conviction and honor stolen by a liar
not a care in the world, my condition so dire.

I was so slick my faults sure I could fix
a warped Felix the cat with my sick bag of tricks.
But I was wrong
I was so very, very wrong
and I was losing my soul…

CHAPTER THREE

HE WHO BEGAN A GOOD WORK

ANOTHER chapter of poetry detailing my perspectives while under God's reconstruction.

Changed - My spiritual "makeover."
(2 Corinthians 5:17)

Why I Need My Wounds - A reason for my trials, tribulations, and sufferings. While the process may be painful at times God is constantly at work in me and works all things together for my own good.
(Romans 8:18) (Philippians 3:10)

Thank You - An expression of gratitude for my spiritual makeover.
(Eph. 5:20)

Sin Shall Not - My true freedom from sin.

(Romans 6:14)

The Greatest is Love - There is nothing greater than God's love despite the teachings of the faith movement I was subjected to in the mid *80's.

(1 Corinthians 13:13)

Dichotomy - Myself in Christ defined in rhymes which are eternal truths rather than contradictions.

(2 Corinthians 5:17)

Changed

You did not change the situation,
You changed me.
You did not change the other person,
You changed me.
You did not change the circumstance,
You changed me.
You did not change the problem,
You changed me.
You did not change the weather,
You changed me.
You did not change my enemy,
You changed me.
You did not my change my family,
You changed me.
You did not change Your mind,
You changed me.
You did not change my finances,
You changed me'
You did not change the traffic light,
You changed me.
Because in all these things what really needed to
change was me.

Why I Need My Wounds

Yes, My son, I've heard your prayer
and know that I am quite aware.
indeed, I do understand how you are feeling
and it may make good sense to ask now for your
healing.
Your wounds and your sufferings are part of this life
so, bear them and share them and work through the
strife...
There are others who need to see how you endure
of My love and My strength help Me make them
quite sure.
My Son and I seek vessels that are not quite whole
the withered, the weak and the downtrodden soul...
Through gaps and holes and fissures quite fine
are the places in you where My Sons Light can
shine.
It is painful and lonely I know that is true
It was painful and lonely for My only Son too...
So stay strong in My Love and I'll tell you well done
then forever you'll live in the peace of My Son.

THANK YOU

You blinded me so I could see
You took the I out of the me.
You broke my wings so I could fly
You took the log out of my eye.
You broke my heart to make it whole
You emptied me to fill my soul.
You broke my crutch so I would lean
You healed my mind and made it clean.
Thank You

SIN SHALL NOT

My sins are so despicable.
My sins I so detest.
My sins I want to leave behind.
I want them off my chest.
They are lie and illusion
to my soul a pollution.
Do they lead me astray
or to the heart of God's mercy?
Does their forgiveness cause me also to forgive?
Do they reveal my inability
or my need for deep humility?
Do they confirm me as bastard
or qualify me as prodigal?
Are they scars on my soul
or the shadows of a former life?
Do they point to my failure
or to the victory of Holy ransom?
Do those which remain
do so for my growth or for my guilt?
I admit I do not know…
Yet there is still hope for me.
Jesus prepares a place.
Sin shall not have dominion over me.
I'm not under law but under grace.

THE GREATEST IS LOVE

Now abide these three things, faith, hope and love,
but the greatest of these is love.
In new boldness, love perfected
by God's Hand I have defected
from the faith movement to the love movement
since of course love is greatest.
If I display my great faith you may be impressed
but if I show you my love you may just be blessed.
And I would rather bless than impress
because this is not about me, my knowledge of The
Word
my spiritual gifts or emotional lifts.
So, thanks but no thanks I don't need to run far or
near
to receive the latest spiritual outpouring
it's all sitting right here
Christ in me. my hope of glory.
As far as I can see
better one moment in the heart of God's love
than all eternity in grand prophetic utterance.

Brother so and so once said
"This love thing is okay, but you must press on

to the deeper things of God!"
My, how odd...
If indeed God is love as it says in First John
could it then be true as we zealously press on
we are pressing right past the truth into excess
where we seek to impress again rather than bless?

Paul the Apostle in a vision so great
humbly remembered his own lowly state.
And instead of a polished and grand presentation
to captivate multitudes and win over the nation,
shared instead of his weaknesses so I could see
that Paul the Apostle was a man much like me.
Or if with my great faith I were to say "Mountain
depart"
but have not the true love of Christ in my heart
I am nothing...but deceived.
So, I'd rather have love that my works truly shine
as Christ within me, not an effort of mine.
Now the love of God controls me, enfolds me.
I grow in the rays of The Sons perfect love devoid of
fear

whose warmth envelopes me as I draw near.
One to one, heart to heart, God to child
the face of Jesus upon me smiled.
And if you dare to believe in His love
there is nothing that can stop its flow.

Not today, not tomorrow, not ever.

DICHOTOMY

I'm as a serpent
as a dove
a soldier
in the war of love.
I am bold
I am meek
I am strongest
when I'm weak.
I'm alive
and yet I'm dead.
I'm made whole
by broken bread.
I'm in the heavens
I'm here as well
And I can stand
because He fell.
I'm a man
but am not male
and I succeed
each time I fail.
I was paid for
yet I'm free

I'm in One
and They are three.
I can see more
through closed eyes.
I rest while running
for the prize.
I find treasures
in life's pain
and deepest pleasures
in things most plain.
I see The Light
in darkest times
and seek out truths
behind riddles and rhymes.

CHAPTER FOUR

JESUS CHRIST

ONE final chapter of my poetry centered on the person, character and nature of Jesus.

You Loved Them - This touching piece stresses the constant, undying love of Christ, even for those who killed Him.

(Luke 23:24)

One Week - Written from the perspective of one of the Apostles, this spellbinding work chronicles the week from the triumphal entry to the crucifixion.

(Mark 14:50) (Matthew 26:75)

Holy Wounds - A unique narrative of the wounds in the hands, feet and side of Jesus if they could speak.

(Isaiah 53:5)

The Revelation - A glorious depiction of the resurrected Christ, taken from Revelation Chapters One and Four.

He Is (Part One) - God said "I Am" therefore, He Is.

(Exodus 3:14)

He Is (Part Two) - Once again, He Is

(Exodus 3:14)

The Gift - A new perspective on Christmas.

(Luke 2:11)

God's Little Lambs - God's little lambs are children of all ages who go to church to find The Great Shepherd and are instead met by people claiming to know God and speak for Him, but do not accurately represent the character, nature, mercy, compassion, and unconditional love of God, but rather their own ego, intolerance and judgment.

(Ezekiel 34:4)

Misunderstood - People very often did

not understand Jesus, His message, or His mission. (Luke 13:34)

Why I Love Jesus - A sincere expression of my adoration and love for the One I belong to, the One who knew me when I was yet in my mothers' belly. The One who loved me, claimed me for His own and purchased me with His blood.

YOU LOVED THEM

You loved the woman at the well.
You loved them as three times You fell.
You loved them as You drank the cup.
You loved when You were lifted up.

You loved them as they struck your face
and as they pierced Your heart.
You loved them as they tore Your beard.
You loved them as they spit and jeered.

You loved them though their witness false.
You loved despite their lies.
You spoke Your love through bleeding lips.
You loved through blackened eyes.

You loved them as they nailed You down.
Into Your head a thorny crown.
You loved them as they spoke profane
blasphemies against Your Name.

You loved them though their hearts they'd harden.
You loved them as You asked their pardon.
You loved them with Your final sigh.
You loved them as You said goodbye.

ONE WEEK

On one Sunday, palms were raised in a reverent
embrace.
On the next, palms were raised to strike the face
of the Holy One, God's only begotten Son.
Who came to us gently, humbly, on a donkey's colt?
Not in pomp, nor in glory.
Couldn't they see Your maternal Jerusalem tears?
How could "Hosanna!" turn to a traitorous "Crucify
Him!" in just days?
Gethsemane Garden now become a trading table
upon which You as the goods were delivered.
We couldn't even stay awake with You
and try to soothe Your fear
as You soaked in a dripping mask of crimson…
"Even if all else forsake You, I will not!
I...I.. I DON'T EVEN KNOW THAT GUY!"
Where were Your friends who in recent days
You had delivered from darkness, silence, torment,
and death?
Where were they?
Where was I?

And You, ripped apart, staked alive, bleeding and
abandoned
on that barren hill of death
we hiding away like scared little mice
each to his own private horror contemplations.
Where had it all gone?
The multitudes, the miracles, the glory
all exchanged for a handful of gawking, gasping
hand over mouth mourners
seeing their hero brought down low, low, low.
The end coming so swiftly, so brutally
not in power but defeat.
Now we cower in retreat.
Doors closed, shades drawn
wondering where it all went wrong.
In one week, everything we had come to believe
had come unraveled and undone.
This was God's only begotten Son?
The dream is now a nightmare.
And You still hanging there
drip, drip, drip,
Why, why, why don't You die?
Why do You suffer and linger?
How could this be happening?

Holy Wounds

We are the Holy Wounds of Jesus Christ.
Through us flows the blood that will
cleanse the nations.
Through hands, feet and side we open up to a
hostile world
to pour out lovingkindness, mercy and forgiveness.
We bear witness to The Christ, The Holy
Kamikazee of love
who on a rescue mission,
offered up His life to become the pincushion of
the devil's hatred.
Our first visions were the hateful faces
of sadistic Roman soldiers inflicting us into His
innocent flesh.
The first sounds we ever heard were His screams of
agony.
We are the hands of Jesus Christ which once only
touched, healed
and gestured explanation of great and mighty
mysteries
hidden from the minds of men from before the
dawn of the age

and we would learn the brutal intrusion of man,
spikes driven through, rendering us useless.
We are the feet of Jesus Christ, which once ushered
Him
from village to village, victim to victim
that He would touch, heal and move on
never to be washed by the bloodstained hands of an
unclean world.
I am the side of Jesus Christ, through me men
pierced the heart
that so desperately wanted to embrace
the very world
that was only interested in running a
spear through it.
We are the Holy Wounds of Jesus Christ.
We marred the form of The Master that you might
be made whole.
We will become the scars of inscription
each of your names written here forever.
Look upon us and know that we are the reminders
of the day
God moved heaven and earth to destroy death
and bestow the gift of life upon fallen creation
and our message is one of mercy, grace, forgiveness
and love.

THE REVELATION

The King of Kings like jasper stone
seated in glory upon a thundering throne
before the throne a crystal sea
stretching to infinity.
An emerald rainbow round.
Twenty-four elders bowing down
all dressed in robes of white.
His shining countenance is their guiding light.
Girded about His once pierced chest a golden band
and holding seven stars within His Holy hand.
His hair and once plucked beard as snow.
From His mouth a two-edged sword did go.
And the living creatures four
Crying "Holy, Holy, Holy" to the One they adore.
They're full of eyes around.
As the twenty-four elders cast their crowns
before the Holy feet once nailed down
now like bronze refined by the fire of His burning
eyes.
As the eternal chorus of a Holy priesthood cries
"You are worthy, O Lord
to receive glory, honor and power

for You created all things
and by Your will they exist and were created!"
With no rest by night or day
the four living creatures say
"Holy, Holy, Holy Lord God Almighty
Who was and is and is to come!"

HE IS (PART ONE)

He is found in the still, quiet place.
He is searching the scared, lonely face.
He is mountain high.
Heard in the infant's cry.
He is all around.
He is the path of life.
Surgeon without a knife.
He is before what was
and after what once will be.
My Savior lives, He cannot die.
The rushing wind is His gentle sigh.
The shallow mind may not understand
those footprints of love
sunken deep in the sand.
He is forever, for now, for you and I.
Heard in the infant's cry.

He Is (Part Two)

Every second of my life depends on God.
He is father time and mother nature.
He is the S-O-N, moon and the stars.
He is the joy, the pain, the sorrow.
He is forever, for now and tomorrow.
He is wonder, hope and peace.
Lion and Lamb.
The ages and the seconds.
He is the trip, the tunnel, the floor and the door.
He is the doctor.
The doctor is in…me.
He is healing.
Oh, so gently self-revealing.
The wellspring of all that is pure.
He alone stands Holy, beautiful.
In brilliant majesty,
Christ The Lord.

THE GIFT

On this December twenty fifth
there is no cake and You're The Gift.
The only Gift that keeps on giving
two thousand years of love.
Tell me Jesus why would You bother
to leave the company of Your Father,
assume the burden of sinless flesh
to come rescue the human mess
and save the little ones who sinned
scattered like leaves on the wind
now raked lovingly homeward.
So on this December twenty fifth
we say Merry Birthday
and we ask The Gift to open us up.

God's Little Lambs

Who'll defend God's little lambs
when the wolves come out to feed?
Moving in upon the flock
predators indeed.
Nails, teeth and wolfen doctrine
all honed razor keen,
appearing oh so spiritual
so pious and so clean.
Inside full of dead man's bones.
Deafened to the poor lamb's moans,
Ripping, tearing infant flesh.
Salivating for a kill that's fresh.
Poor little lambs needing to be fed…instead…
of fed upon.
Who'll defend God's little lambs?
Who will lead them home?
Who will lead them in and out
to open pasture free from doubt
who will teach them to cry out
when they are struck and wounded?
Who will teach them who they are
who Jesus is

about the scars
upon His hands and feet and side
and why Jesus was crucified.
and oftentimes how Jesus cried…
because there was no one to defend God's little
lambs

MISUNDERSTOOD

You were a wanderer in leather sandals.
They tried to force You to become their king.
You would not get involved in worldly scandals.
Politics You did not come to bring.

A King You are indeed O Lord of heaven.
But not such as people would suppose.
A devil twelfth among Your true eleven.
Why You called him friend only heaven knows.

You often went alone unto the mountain.
With Your Father You sought to be alone.
Living Water from a Living Fountain.
With every breath You tried to make Him known.

You were the first to call The Lord our Father.
Yourself You called our Brother and our Friend.
With pretentious ritual You would not bother.
Comfort was the precious gift You left to send.

They rarely saw the truth behind Your meaning.
It's hard to see the pure through impure eyes.

So why wake up when you prefer dreaming.
It's hard to see The Son through cloudy skies.

What was it like when they just would not hear
You?
Your words the keys that would set them all free.
From open prison cells they'd not draw near You.
With open arms You said "Come unto Me."

Young John knew with his head at rest upon You.
That invitation stands for us today.
So many seem to look so far beyond You.
But we still need You Lord, You are The Way.

What was it like for them to turn from You and
leave You?
Did Your heart break so it split You open wide?
So many of Your own did not receive You.
And just who gave You comfort when You cried?.

Looking down upon them from the death tree.
I have to feel Your heart was breaking too.
Your innocence surrendered to set them free.
Forgiving words "They know not what they do."

Jesus you are The One there is no other.

Your tender mercies every morning new.
Please show me how to be Your friend and brother
and for eternity I'll always be with You.

WHY I LOVE JESUS

I will begin by quoting from First John Chapter Four verse nineteen "…we love Him because He first loved us." How would I know love and how else could I love had God not placed the design of His great love within me? Apart from Him I can do nothing. So how do I love Jesus? Let me count the ways. I love Him for giving me the ability to love Him back and to love my brother who I have seen. I love Him for who He is, who He has made me and what He has done.

I love him for His supreme and ultimate act of love, His brave, selfless, sacrificial death upon the cross at Calvary because greater love has no one than to lay one's life down for His friends. I love Him because for the joy set before Him He endured the cross, hating the shame while wearing the thorns of my curse upon His brow. I love Him for His ministry of reconciliation and His constant intercession on my behalf before The Father. I love my High Priest who sympathizes with all my weaknesses. I love Him for the gentle ways in which He reveals Himself to me. I love Him for the comfort of His presence which melts calamity and and assures me that no matter what I experience, everything is and will be alright. For the songs of deliverance, he sings to me and the song of gladness He has placed in my soul. For a relationship so unique it escapes description and cannot be completely shared with others yet speaks in its silence louder than thunder. I love Him for giving me not what I deserve but rather the desire of my heart which He Himself has become. I love Him for His tender mercies which are new every morning and for sanctuary so serene it is more renewing than sleep. I love Him for making me accepted in the beloved after being rejected by the world. I love Him for being The Rock of my Salvation on whom and in whom I rest securely. For the way I am fearfully and wonderfully made and the good health He has mercifully kept me in. I love Him for the beauty of His creation as revealed in nature and for the perfect order of the seasons which change and remain the same as His spoken word has set them in motion. I love Him for the conviction and correction He lovingly bestows upon me while always remaining the great preserver of my dignity. I love Him because he desires my invitations rather than my promises. I love Him for the four hundred and ninety-one times a day He mercifully forgives me my trespasses, for never going fishing in His sea of forgetfulness, for casting all my sins behind His back and never turning around and for the east remaining just as far from the west.

I love Him because He is intimately concerned with every aspect of my life and every fiber of my being. He is the author and finisher of my faith and will perfect that which concerns me. I love Him for the tears we have shed together through years of pain, staying closer than a brother, never removing from my shoulders the loving arms which have carried me even to this day. I love Him for placing me in His eye of the hurricane, beneath the shelter of His wings and for hiding me in the secret place of His Tabernacle. I love Him for giving me His heart when my own was cold, hard, worn out and broken. I love Him for removing my corruption and restoring my innocence. He is my Father and my Mother, my Brother and my best friend, the true lover of my soul. I love Him because I may always come to Him as I am, without pretense and even boldly. I love Him for His ear which is continuously inclined to me as He desires my constant communication. I love Him that I may look at Him alone and not at anything else lest I become discouraged, depressed, bitter, cynical, lonely or arrogant and that I may be myself with Him who is more intimately acquainted with my being than even I am and that the real me is hidden with Christ in God and that it is only by looking at Him I can even begin to see who I truly am, who He has created me to be.

I love Him for His deep joy, which is my strength, His glory which is my rear guard, for He Himself who is my peace and for that peace which surpasses understanding. I love Him because in Him I am complete, lacking nothing. I am forever lovingly indebted to The One who reached down and picked me up when I lay naked, broken, filthy, starving and fed me from His Holy hand, washed me with His tears, healed me with His Spirit and clothed me with His robe of righteousness. How do I love Jesus? It is impossible to count the ways.

CHAPTER FIVE

WALKING IT OUT DAILY

Fear and Worry - My conclusions regarding the years I spent trapped in these two lies and illusions and the unnecessary, self-imposed traumas I subjected myself to as a result. Both are contrary to the faith and peace God always had for me to walk in.

(Isaiah 41:10) (Matt. 6:27)

Sufferings - An overview of this universal aspect in our lives and how randomly pointless and cruel they can seem when viewed apart from God's greater purpose in and for them.

(Philippians 3:10)

Surrender : The Battlefield of the Mind - A look at the necessary process of yielding described by John the Baptist "He must

increase but I must decrease." (John 3:30)
and the apostle Paul "I die daily."

(1 Corinthians 15:31)

Voices : There are many voices vying for our
attention. One of them leads to life, peace
and victory, the other leads to chaos, confu-
sion and defeat. The contrast between the
two is as stark as day and night, yet we can
still get confused.

(John 10:27)

Helpful Scriptures - A collection of scriptures
which have been a source of strength and
peace for me over the years through times of
trial, angst and difficulty.

FEAR AND WORRY

BECAUSE God loves and cares for me more than I can understand, because I have asked Him to heal me and conform me to the image of His Son and because at times, I am truly a helpless mess. He has shown me that some levels of fear within me run deeper than I am aware of. They have held me back and held me captive. They have been part of my psyche for so long, I blindly accept them and try to live my life around them the same way I would if I were dragging a dinosaur's tail behind me. I worry about the things I'm afraid of like the health and safety of my family, disease, death, the future, finances, being judged, rejected, unloved or ending up being alone which with God is impossible. As God shows me these things, I become more aware of how well He knows me (better than I know myself), how intimately He is acquainted with me, how much He loves me, how merciful He's been to me, how deep and lasting is His commitment to me and the depth of healing He wants to bring to me. These all help create a deeper love, trust, and devotion within me toward Jesus who is my God, my brother, and my best friend.

I grow in confidence that His thoughts toward me are of peace and not of evil, to give me a future and a hope." (Jeremiah 11:29) I realize that throughout my entire life He has not only seen everything going on around me, but also everything going on within me, which He is far more concerned with. I am in awe of God who is everything he says He is because he is not a liar. He is doing all the things I have asked Him to do with my life, not just in the ways I supposed. He knows best so I must trust Him and endure. I don't want to talk the talk then shrink away like a hypocrite and coward. Perhaps one day the stakes will be even higher, and something will be required of me that through lack of faith and trust I would not be willing to lay down. I don't know. What I do know is that our God is a good God. He is who He says He is, and I believe Him because in Him there is only truth.

SUFFERINGS

IN Phillipians 3:10 Paul writes "...that I may know Him, the power of His resurrection, and the fellowship of His sufferings..." We hear a lot about the power of His resurrection but not so much about the fellowship of His sufferings. The fellowship of sufferings is something to be shared, to partake of together. So, if we are to walk in the fullness of Christ, we must come to know suffering. It is human nature to want to avoid suffering, and I don't believe God has created a life of suffering for us, but rather a life full of His beauty and joy sometimes during suffering. Hebrews 5:8 says of Jesus : "...although He were a Son, yet He learned obedience through the things he suffered." Suffering can birth two offspring, compassion, or bitterness.

When we suffer with God, we birth patience and compassion. When we suffer apart from Him, we birth hate and bitterness. This offspring can either sustain or destroy us. One is a treasure from darkness, the other is a corrosive cancer which corrupts the soul. The choice lies ever present before us. There is no wall tall enough, no bank account full enough, no drug that can make one high enough and no seat powerful enough to enable one to escape suffering. The slickest tongue sticks like glue, the smoothest move grates like sandpaper, the best laid plans of mice avail more than those of men and in the end, we are left with just ourselves and God.

As suffering comes to us all in one form or another, we can be molded into the gentle, yielding, humble, unselfish image of Christ or we can morph into what we become apart from Him. In times of suffering if we turn from God, we turn from our only true source of comfort. It is far better to suffer with Him. Psalm 56:8 tells us that God fills His bottle with the tears we cry in this life. In my case, He could fill not a bottle but an ocean. If you have not yet suffered in your lifetime, you may not understand what I am saying. Be that as it may, rest assured that no matter what we face here, if we endure the refining fire of godly suffering, joy unspeakable awaits us.

SURRENDER; THE BATTLEFIELD OF THE MIND

THE mind is where it all happens. It is the battlefield upon which we work out our salvation and become conformed to the image of Christ. It is the place we combat our negative thoughts, fears, worries and weaknesses. It is a lifelong process during which God never lets go of our hand. 1 Corinthians 2:16 says "...we have the mind of Christ." God wants to continually guide our thoughts. The words "In Him and In Christ" are a repeated theme throughout the New Testament. 2 Corinthians 5:17 says ``If anyone be in Christ, they are a new creation, old things have passed away and all things have become new." Acts 17:28 says "In Him we live and move and have our being." Colossians 2:10 says "...we are complete in Him..." So how do we access being in Him or in Christ? I believe it is through surrender. Not giving up a few things here or there we know God doesn't approve of but total, complete, lay my down life surrender.

We must fully give up on ourselves so to speak. Fully give up on our way of thinking, our desires, convictions, presuppositions, perceptions, assumptions, etc. and allow ourselves to be completely absorbed into the character and nature of God. Paul described it as dying to self. In fact, he went as far as to say, "I die daily." We die to our old nature, our self-image. our pride, our ego, our rights, etc. He replaces our minds with His. We learn to clothe ourselves in Christ. Ephesians 6:13 says to "put on the full armor of God." It details the weapons of war worn by Roman soldiers. Each piece of the armor represents Christ, such as the helmet of salvation which guards our minds. Our focus isn't on a helmet but on Christ who is the Rock of our salvation and paid for it with His precious blood. The breastplate of righteousness which guards our hearts points our focus to Jesus who is Himself our righteousness. The shield of faith speaks to our faith in Him alone and His finished work on the cross which dispels the lies, the fiery darts of the devil. The sword of the spirit (an offensive weapon) which is the Word of God, Jesus being The Word made flesh. The belt of truth as Jesus said, "I am the way, the truth and the life." And finally, our feet stand firmly on the gospel of peace. Ephesians 2:14 tells us that Jesus Himself is our peace. So that is the spiritual, emotional, and psychological safety our armor provides. We stand in the knowledge that we are completely covered and that He Himself is our salvation, our righteousness, and the epicenter of our faith. He is the Word alive within us, our guiding truth and the peace that surpasses our understanding. So, it's by surrendering our sense of self while abandoning the mechanisms we have devised apart from Him and taking Himself upon us as our spiritual armor that we do battle and stand strong no matter what befalls us. We are no longer subjected to the limited mandates of our own which will leave us forever trapped in fear, worry, doubt, uncertainty etc. because we have died to those things and are therefore no longer subject to them. I hearken back to 2 Cor. 5:17 "If anyone be in Christ they are a new creation, old things have passed away and all things have become new," As I said, this is a lifelong process during which God never lets go of our hand.

VOICES

"**STOP** being fake. You haven't changed. People don't really like you. You could never accomplish that. Who do you think you are? You're different from everybody else. You don't fit in. Stop trying to be something you're not. Give up. Quit now 'cuz it'll never work. People see right through you. How can you call yourself a Christian? You are unacceptable to God. There's something about you that keeps God from helping you. These people are all Christians but not you. If people ever find out what you're really like they wouldn't have anything to do with you. You still have a bad temper. You still have lustful thoughts. No one else thinks those kinds of things. If you were really saved, you wouldn't think that or say that or do that etc....." And those lies go on and on and on in many of our heads. Same script for lots of believers day after day, week after week, month after month, year after year. Those lies shut you down and shut you out. They keep you on the outside looking in. They keep you from feeling a sense of belonging and from growing into being who you truly are. They are designed to hold you hostage and mute so they can remain unshared. unspoken and unbroken. Don't listen to them. The devil has a very limited repertoire yet it's still effective. It's effective because we don't call him out on it. They create fear in us, so we don't share them and let them remain secret. We are silently fearful that his lies are the truth when they are not. They are illusions, specters, phantoms, bluffs and substance less accusations. God's word says the opposite about us than those lies. It tells us we are accepted in the beloved, that we can do all things through Christ who strengthens us, that no weapon formed against us will prosper, that He who began a good work in us will complete it, that we are His workmanship created in Christ Jesus unto good works, that our names were written in The Lamb's Book of Life from before the foundation of the world, that He is in us to work and to will according to His good pleasure, that He loves us with an everlasting love and so on.

But somehow the lies can sound like thunder in our minds at times while God's words are a whisper. They're a whisper because he speaks in a still, small voice. In John 10:27 Jesus said "My sheep hear My voice; I know them, and they follow Me." Psalm 46:10 says, "Be still and know that I am God." Being still is the only way we can know. We can't know by fretting, worrying, panicking, and being allowed to be made paranoid. I speak of these things as someone who has dealt with and still deals with them. But as I grow in Christ, the lies grow fainter and God's whispers grow louder. I begin to discern that which causes me to doubt myself, God and His word is from the enemy and that which builds me up in Christ is from The Lord. I choose to believe the truth which is Christ Himself. I choose to believe the things He says about Himself in me are eternally true and not subject to change. I realize I have an enemy whose mission is to create doubt and fear within me. An enemy who seeks to fill me with a false sense of guilt and feelings of inadequacy. An enemy whose arsenal consists of lies and illusions and is counting on me to fall for them as the only power his lies have is the power, I give them by not believing the truth of God's word. We must be careful of which voices we heed as both speak to us constantly. We are in a battle. And the battle takes place in our minds as I have written previously in this chapter. The great news is the battle is already won and Christ is The Victor. It is our heritage to walk in the victory He has given us and it does not include being tormented by lies.

Helpful Scriptures

Matthew 11:28-30 - "Come to Me all you who labor and are heavily burdened and I will give you rest. Take My yoke upon you and learn from Me, for I am gentle and humble in spirit and in Me you will find rest for your souls. For My yoke is easy and my burden is light."

Proverbs 3:5-6 - "Trust in The Lord with all your heart and lean not on your own understanding. In all your ways acknowledge Him and He will direct your path."

Jeremiah 29:11 - "For I know the thoughts I think toward you says The Lord, thoughts of peace and not of evil. To give you a future and a hope."
Isaiah 26:3 "You will keep him in perfect peace whose mind is stayed on You.

Ephesians 2:14 - "For He Himself is our peace...""

1 Peter 5:7 - "Cast your anxiety on Him because He cares for you."

Philippians 4:6 - "Be anxious for nothing, but in all things by prayer and supplication with thanksgiving let your requests be made known to God, and the peace of God which surpasses understanding, will keep your hearts and minds in Christ Jesus."

Isaiah 41:40 - "Do not fear for I am with you, do not be dismayed for I am your God. Surely, I will strengthen you and help you. I will uphold you with My righteous right hand

2 Timothy 1:7 - "For God has not given us a spirit of fear, but of power, of love and a sound mind."

1 John 4:18 - "There is no fear in love, but perfect love casts out fear…"

Isaiah 43:1 - "Thus says The Lord who created you and He who formed you. Fear not for I have redeemed you, I have called you by name. You are Mine.""

CHAPTER SIX

A FEW SHORT STORIES

HITCHHIKING STORIES

DURING my teen years in the 70's, I did a lot of hitchhiking. In those days you would see an occasional hitchhiker, now it's unheard of. Hitchhikers are an extinct species. I hitchhiked locally and once hitchhiked to Florida, which you can read about in My Story. Not only was hitchhiking my normal mode of transportation, but I also hitched recreationally. Sometimes when I had nothing to do, I would head out to Ocean Avenue which ran the length of the Jersey Shore from Highlands to Seaside Heights, hook out a thumb and fish for adventure. When I reflect on the cast of characters and situations I encountered, I see God at work both protecting me and making introductions. There was a biker who witnessed to me about Jesus. There was another biker who pulled out a knife, only to shrug and put it away when God had me react with aggression. There was the narcoleptic Orthodox Jewish guy who kept falling asleep at the wheel. There was the van door that opened, revealing a cargo full of angry looking gang bangers. There was the car that swerved at me and pulled over after I gave them an unfriendly gesture. I ran toward the car, reaching into my pocket as though I had a gun, daring them to get out. After a few tense moments they called my bluff, jumped out and the chase was on, but God helped me escape. I was once given a lift by Clarence Clemons, the saxophone player in Bruce Springsteen's band and we had a great discussion about God. There was the time I couldn't get a ride, so I grabbed a pair of crutches someone was throwing out at the curb and used them to get picked up almost immediately. The people were so kind that I felt horribly guilty. There were local bands coming from late night gigs. There were lots of friendly, partying girls. There was the tractor trailer incident which you can read about in My Story as well. There were well-intentioned drivers, perverts, people using and sharing drugs and even a couple of little old ladies. I know that without God's hand of protection any number of horrible things could have happened to me. Many people have disappeared hitchhiking. That's why I thank Him for His merciful protection because without Him, I too may have disappeared. So, thank you Jesus for keeping Your holy hand on a reckless little wildman from the Jersey Shore. Thank you for loving me and saving me from sin, death, hell, and myself. Thank you, King of the universe, for Your tender mercies

which are new every morning and Your great faith-
fulness. Thank you for making me. Thank you for
making me Your own. Thank you for making me live
even when I wanted to die. And thanks for the rides!

THE GEESE

"Draw near to God and He will draw near
to you…"

(James 4:8)

I have always been a lover of both animals and
nature. I used to enjoy feeding the geese in the
fall when they would stop over at a local pond during
migration. One thing I noticed during my times
feeding them was that some of the geese were willing
to get closer to me than others. I don't know if they
were hungrier, more trusting, or more intelligent
but at any rate the ones that came closer I fed more
than those that stayed further away. Some were even
willing to feed from my hand and they got the most
food. Then I realized that a parallel between the geese
and God's children was staring me right in the face.
The same dynamic plays out in our relationship with
Him. Those who draw nearer to God are fed more
while those who remain farther away are fed less.
Had the geese which remained a distance away from
me moved closer, I certainly would have fed them
more as well. But for some reason (which I suspect

was fear) they did not. I believe God wants to feed each of us more and more of Himself and how much of Him we receive is directly connected to how close to Him we draw. I want to draw as close to Him as I possibly can so He can feed me in greater and greater quantities. I want to strive to be like the geese which fed from my hand and receive all the fullness God has for me.

Another thing I noticed by observing the geese was that some served as what I call "watchers." While the other geese fed with their heads down to the ground, the watchers stood on the edges of the perimeter of the flock, necks extended and heads held high on the alert, scanning for predators. I found this interesting and saw a parallel to the body of Christ. We can and should serve as watchers for one another, remaining on alert, scanning for the threats and schemes of the evil one, protecting, warning, and alerting one another. In doing so we become a protective barrier for the body of Christ as a whole. And the cool thing is that we don't have to fly south to do it.

THE DEATH OF SNOWFLAKE

SNOWFLAKE was Mrs. Hartsgrove's West Highland Terrier. Tiny, fluffy and white with big brown eyes, Snowflake was as adorable as he could be. Every morning at six o'clock Mrs. Hartsgrove would let Snowflake out into her fenced in yard where he would sit like a little sentinel by the gate and bark incessantly at each bird, squirrel or person passing by. Snowflake's bark was a shrill yip-yap that would pierce the tranquil morning air like a stinger missile. Sometimes Mrs. Hartsgrove would be in the yard with Snowflake continually imploring him to be quiet. But the little guy would simply ignore her impotent requests to cease and desist and continue yipping and yapping if not at the birds, squirrels, or passersby, then at the gentle breeze.

Yip yap, yip yap, yip yap all day every day. This went on for years and years. Then one morning there was a strange quiet in the neighborhood. Something was missing. Where was Snowflakes' yip yapping? Sadly, enough I came to learn that Snowflake, the adorable little tormenting harpy had passed away during the night.

I went over and consoled Mrs. Hartsgrove as best I could, assuring her that she'd see her beloved Snowflake again one day in heaven. And I'm sure she will. In fact, I'd bet that right now Snowflake is sitting at heavens' gate just as he sat at Mrs. Hartsgrove's gate, shredding the peace and quiet by incessantly yipping and yapping at the angels passing by and ignoring Saint Peters' repeated requests for him to cease and desist. May God bless little Snowflake.

Aslan Youth
Ministries

"Out of the Mouths of Babes"

(Psalm 8:2)

ONE of the greatest privileges of my life has been serving on staff as a youth minister and as a volunteer with Aslan Youth Ministries. Its founders are Craig and Lynn Ann Bogard. If we were ever going to send anyone to another planet to show them what true Christians are like, it would be Craig and Lynn Ann.

Originally from Texas where Craig was studying to become a doctor in the early 70's, they heard God's voice and followed it to Tinton Falls, New Jersey where they still live in the house in the woods they built with their own hands. They started an outreach ministry to underprivileged children and families there and expanded it into several surrounding towns and eventually into Haiti. I've taught bible class, helped coach the basketball team, drove the big blue Aslan bus, and helped with the food pantry and clothing distribution programs. One afternoon in bible class I asked my group of kids to recite their weekly bible verse. One little boy named Theodore informed me that he was suddenly suffering from an upset stomach and would not be able to recite his verse. He asked if he could go lie down on the couch in one of the empty classrooms. I said, "Sure Theo, but first let's say a quick prayer for you." So, we prayed that God would heal his stomach.

After class ended, the children were running around outside on the playground as usual when I happened to spot Theo scooting up the ladder and down the slide, smiling and laughing with his friends. I walked over and said, "Theo you were so sick a little while ago, what happened?" The guilty look on his face told the whole story. Suddenly he smiled and said, "Yeah but we prayed!" He got me and I had to laugh aloud. He smiled as he went to take his turn climbing up the ladder once more. I walked away, realizing that this moment was a pure blessing and that sometimes it is best to throw the rulebook away so that the greater lessons can be learned about innocence, mercy & God's love.

False Intro :
Backsliding and
Repentance

MY initial introduction to Christianity came in the mid 1980's during the height of the prosperity gospel. This theology conflicted deeply with what was in my heart and soul. In time it sent me away utterly disillusioned, full of bitterness and feeling had. So, I retreated to the only life I knew, one of self-destruction and sin. In the aberrant prosperity theology, God became a genie of the lamp so to speak and with the proper spiritual formulation, would bend to your will and provide you with whatever it was you desired. This false gospel depended on faith in your will not in Christ Himself. The power came not from the Holy Spirit but from the strength of your desire to obtain that which you wanted. It was carnal, self-indulgent, and materialistic. In other words, it was completely satanic. Apostate televangelists became immensely wealthy during this time and there was no shortage of heretics seen on Christian television networks. It exalted the love of money, the root of all kinds of evil. But I read Matthew 8:20 which said, "Birds have nests and foxes have holes, but The Son of Man has no place to rest His head." John 13:35 said "By this all men will know you are My disciples, if you have love for one another."

The prosperity gospel claimed that people would know you were a child of God by your financial wealth and amount of material possessions. Were it not for a minister named Wayne Monbleau and his radio program "Let's Talk About Jesus", I may very well have given up on the pursuit of God altogether and died in my sins. Thankfully, Wayne's teachings centered on God's love and remained a thread which kept me connected to Jesus. He was and still is a minister of grace and truth. When I walked in fellowship with God, I was spiritually sound and lived uprightly but when I backslid, I was dark, angry, and depraved as well as sexually and chemically addicted. I was a skilled con artist with an uncanny ability to detect people's egos and use their egos against them for my own selfish gain. I would also appeal to their sense of kindness or decency and would use that to my advantage as well. I began viewing pornography during that time and my mind became a theater of the twisted and bizarre as I exploited others as well as myself.

Thankfully, I never developed the destructive addiction to pornography that sank its evil claws into so many other souls. It warps the human mind and creates a lens of corruption through which all of life is viewed. The common thread in the lives of every serial killer as they have openly and freely admitted is an addiction to pornography. It is one of the devil's most useful and effective tools. Even after delivered from sexual addiction, a person's memory can remain infected by their former behaviors, and it can take many years for their minds to be cleansed and restored.

I stubbornly continued in my life of sin and rebellion until I hit two impenetrable walls. The first wall occurred in 2007 when I contracted a disease called Lentigo which I detail in the beginning of this book in the section called "The Mask." The second wall occurred more recently in 2021 when diagnosed with non-Covid double pneumonia of both lungs, sepsis, malnutrition, and dehydration which I almost did not survive. But I did survive by God's immeasurable grace and given one more chance to live the rest of my life as it should be lived, by following His Word and seeking His will. I suffered in plenty of other ways throughout my rebellious years including depression, loneliness, poverty, and despair. But sin being the driving force in my life, kept me from submitting my will to God and continuing in myself destructive course. It was a matter of life and death. Not just physical death but far more importantly a spiritual death that leads to eternal separation from God and a level of suffering for which we have no frame of reference.

The thought of eternal separation from God scares me to my core therefore I must redeem the time I have left. I must make the most of each moment despite the doldrums, distractions, and frequent absurdities of each day. I now view each passing one as an opportunity to create the eternity of my choosing. I know if I keep my focus on Jesus, I will be fine and I will finish my race. I will leave this life and enter His glory rather than my own eternal shame. I will leave redeemed by Him rather than condemned by my sins. I pray that through His strength I will cling to Him and that He will lead and guide my steps until He calls me home. I live daily with hope in the grace and mercy of God my Father who made me part of His heavenly family instead of allowing me to become orphaned in hell.

CONCLUSION

IN my life I have walked with and away from God. It is far better to walk with Him. As suffering comes to us all, we can either be molded into the gentle, yielding, unselfish image of Christ or we can morph into what we become apart from Him. I have had both highs and lows with and without God. Without Him, the lows are deadly, and the highs are disappointing. With Him, the lows are lessons, and the highs are wonderful beyond description. In times of suffering, if we turn from God we turn from our only true source of comfort. It is far better to suffer with Him. Psalm 56:8 tells us that God fills His bottle with our tears. In my case he could fill an ocean. Nevertheless, know that God is The Great Preserver of your dignity, The Great Psychologist of your mind and The Great Lover of your soul. When I look back at my life, I must ask two questions, how and why. How did I survive all those insane things that happened to me and why am I still alive? Regarding the former, I attribute it completely to God's mercy. As to the latter, I suspect it is connected to my sharing with people all that I have to offer, which are the lessons I have learned about the importance of God's presence in my life, even at times when I had forgotten all about Him. Overall, it's the life I've lived. I don't know what else to say. We live on the edge of many precipices. God is our comfort.

A Word of Thanks

I'D like to give a word of thanks to two people who have helped me grow over the years in my spiritual walk. They are Mike Yencarelli and Bob Gonzo. I met Mike twenty-five years ago and he is like a spiritual older brother. He opened his home to me in both hospitality and fellowship. He is the most zealous believer I have ever met, with a heart of love and genuine compassion. As Timothy learned from Paul's living example, so I have learned from Mike. Bob was smiling when I met him thirty years ago and is still smiling today. He has been steadfast in guiding me over the years, sacrificing countless hours of time over the phone listening to my cares, worries, questions, complaints and never once lost patience or made me feel like a burden. I have been tremendously blessed that Jesus placed both Godly men in my life. They have been instrumental in my journey and have helped me get to where I am today. Thank you so much Jesus, for my dear brothers Mike and Bob.

Doxology of Jude

"**N**OW to Him who is able to keep you from stumbling and to present you faultless before the Presence of His glory with exceeding joy, to God our Savior who alone is wise, be glory and majesty, dominion and power, both now and forever, Amen."

Information Page

TO contact Tim regarding speaking engage-
ments, questions, comments, or nutritional
consultation, please use the email address or phone
number provided below. You can also join him on
Instagram or on his Facebook page "Jesus Christ is
our Brother and Lord"

Timothy P. Belford
tpbelford@yahoo.com
848-219-2863

Made in the USA
Las Vegas, NV
26 August 2022

54024214R10063